BECOMING A CARING MANAGER

Bring out the best in your team

Written by Karima Chibane
Translated by Rebecca Neal

Coaching 50MINUTES.com

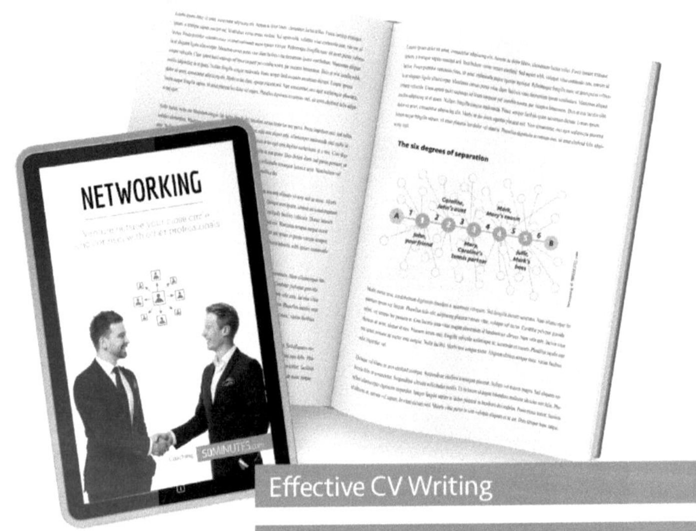
50MINUTES.com

PROPEL
YOUR BUSINESS FORWARD!

Effective CV Writing

Resolving Office Conflict

Boost Your Concentration

Find Your Work-Life Balance

www.50minutes.com

FURTHER READING   36

BECOMING A CARING AND CONGRUENT MANAGER

- **Issue:** how can I manage intergenerational teams in a constantly changing world while looking out for employees' wellbeing?
- **Uses:** caring management increases wellbeing at work and enables the development of synergies through collective intelligence, an increase in performance and creativity, and the prevention of psychosocial risks.
- **Professional context:** management of teams, human resources, talent management, professional relationships, etc.
- **FAQs:**
  - What can I say to people who think that being caring is being naïve?
  - Why should I choose a caring management style directed towards congruence?
  - What are the three key indicators of a caring and congruent approach to management?
  - What is the difference between ethical management, slow management and management-coaching?
  - Is caring a key to happiness in the professional world?
  - How can I become a caring and congruent manager?
  - Can all managers become caring?
  - What do the latest findings about this management style say?

    "All truth passes through three stages. First, it is ridiculed. Second, it is violently opposed. Third, it is accepted as self-evident." (Arthur Schopenhauer)

New ways of managing appear on a regular basis. The trend towards caring management seems more important than most. It began in the USA, like most management trends, before making its way to Europe. The Collins English Dictionary defines "caring" as "feeling or showing care and compassion". In practice, this means looking for the positive in another person or in a situation. Managers must therefore learn to manage their relationships with others in a positive way, in order to achieve effective collective action, which is conducive to higher performance.

However, some managers still too often prioritise numbers, forgetting human relationships and the importance of balance. Interprofessional relationships should nonetheless not be managed mechanically: the limits of this approach have become clear, and the current spike in cases of burnout is a clear symptom of this.

The refocusing of managerial thought on human relationships ahead of the task to be accomplished can now be seen in managerial literature, training courses in management schools, universities, and interventions in consultancy and coaching firms.

The world-renowned Academy of Management (AOM), the largest academic body in the field of management science, took "Dare to Care" as the theme of its 2010 Annual Meeting. Two years later, the *Academy of Management Review* (AMR), a journal published by the AOM and one of the most prestigious journals in the field of business and management, followed this with a dossier on caring management and regular articles on the development of this approach to management.

This surge in interest in the topic of caring and congruence is becoming vitally important. It attracts reflections on ethical management, emotional and interpersonal intelligence, integrity, collective intelligence, agility and slow management. For some, caring management oriented towards congruence is the characteristic of great managers, meaning those who have an assertive personality and are self-confident and open-minded.

CARING MANAGEMENT: THE BASICS

THE MANAGERS OF THE PAST AND THE MANAGERS OF TODAY

What is a manager?

There is a relative consensus between different management authors with regard to the definition of a manager. Their main characteristic lies in their task, namely knowing how to manage and coordinate a group of individuals whom they are responsible for. The director of a company is therefore also a manager.

> **N.B.**
>
> The decision to not distinguish between managers and directors in this guide is deliberate. Caring management can be a shared stance, as each individual has the purpose of creating collective intelligence through synergy.

The manager of tomorrow

The function of management theories is to interpret how organisations work. The first work in this field is relatively recent, as it dates from the start of the 20th century, and it aims to improve the performance of companies.

Until the 1970s, organisations were structured around a bureaucratic model: a strict hierarchy, a substantial degree of control, and little delegation. In this context, the 1990s were a turning point: status and level in the hierarchy were no longer enough, and management turned towards the concept of results and the means of achieving results. Managers had to change: they now needed to develop legitimacy based on relationships. Their ability to motivate their teams began to be prioritised over technical mastery of their job. They had to have strong communication skills as they were thrown into the heart of human relationships and human issues, most of the time with no preparation. This period also saw the globalisation of the markets, increasingly rapid changes of environment and new organisations in networks or in the planning stage.

This paradigm shift for managers led them to activate other resources. Relationship training became necessary, in particular in order to develop empathy and an awareness of emotional intelligence. Managers became leaders. Hard power, the prerogative of aggressive managers and very hierarchical and centralised companies, was over. Although it was suitable in the context of mass production, in our post-industrial society where the mobilisation of intelligence is important and where involvement has replaced obedience, workers are free individuals and display little loyalty towards companies. 'Generation Y' clearly represents this movement, which is structural and will become more pronounced with Generation Z.

- **Generation X** comprises people born between 1960 and 1980. They struggled to find stable and well-paid jobs and tend to remain in their post and climb the professional ladder over time. This generation prioritises the balance between professional and private life. For them, information is slow and controlled. They struggle to understand Generation Y and vice versa.
- **Generation Y** comprises people born between 1980 and 1995. They grew up with television, the development of the internet and video games. For these digital natives, authority does not necessary mean competence. They question everything, including existing approaches to management, which Generation X does not like at all. Generation Y prioritises efficiency over years of experience, and they want to be understood. For them, work is not the most important thing: they are looking for a better quality of life, think in the short term and move around a lot. They want rapid career progression, flexible hours, freedom and independence.
- **Generation Z** comprises people born from 1995 onwards. This generation grew up with social networks and is constantly connected. Unlike other generations, they never experienced life without new technologies. For them, congruence is all the more important considering that soon there will probably be no more barriers between

personal life and professional life, which tend to blend together.

The leader who has well-developed interpersonal intelligence and who adopts a caring and congruent managerial stance is therefore the manager of tomorrow.

WHAT IS CARING AND CONGRUENT MANAGEMENT?

KEYWORDS

- **Ontological security:** the fact of having confidence in one's own being. This feeling of security serves as a solid base to remain centred. It allows individuals to act with respect for themselves and others, rather than reacting according to their defence mechanisms. It opens them to assertiveness. To sum up, for a manager it means being comfortable in their skin, in their role and in the complexity of their environment. This facilitates congruence.
- **Congruence:** the alignment and perfect consistency of thoughts, words and actions. For managers, this can be summed up as: "Doing what you say and saying what you do". This inner harmony makes the individual open to empathy.
- **Empathy:** the possibility for the manager to feel what a worker might be feeling in a time of difficulty or conflict. Empathy is not sympathy, which

comforts people and wraps them in emotion; on the contrary, it is neutral and distant. It is the ability to put yourself in another person's shoes in order to feel what they feel and understand them better, not to make yourself liked.

- **Meaning:** the search for meaning is important today, and is propagated in particular by Generation Y. All the studies show that it is vital to give meaning to the teams you manage.
- **Agility:** the search to continually enhance the development resulting from the collective intelligence of the teams which practice it. For the manager, it means valuing this collective intelligence and promoting mutual trust in order to stimulate, mobilise and coordinate it.

Caring and congruent management involves going back to the heart of the manager's role, as well as finding coherence between personal values and economic efficiency. Caring and congruent management is a way of managing teams based on courtesy. It comprises twelve main points.

1. **Knowing how to listen.** Active listening allows discrepancies between verbal and nonverbal communication to be identified. We now know that in communication, the verbal channel only carries 20-30% of the message. Interpreting body language through the voice, gestures or facial expressions is essential because it provides the essential aspects of the information.
2. **Giving meaning to the work of each colleague.** The idea

is to share an overall vision with everyone, to define tasks clearly and to encourage and recognise everybody's work. It is important to hold regular feedback sessions to get back on the right track if necessary. Of course, this also requires facing up to difficulties and talking about them, with the aim of looking for a shared solution.

3. **Looking out for the wellbeing of individuals,** by putting into place a deliberate and concrete policy which involves employees in the choice of the tools to work with and the working environment. It is also necessary to pay attention to the balance between professional life and personal life by offering the possibility of teleworking or flexible hours, for example.

4. **Improving workers' shared existence** through higher quality relationships. To do this, the manager can, for example, undertake training in emotional intelligence in order to improve their interpersonal skills. Indeed, relationships are at the heart of the managerial role as it is conceived today.

5. **Valuing expression and recognising people's right to make mistakes,** especially during the learning process. When the manager acknowledges their own mistakes in front of their colleagues, they give them permission to do the same. They establish the possibility of learning from mistakes and, consequently, of daring to try innovative ways of doing things. The concept of FailCon, launched in the USA, is a major source of inspiration in this domain.

<u>**DID YOU KNOW?**</u>

FailCon is a conference for startup founders, entrepreneurs and others involved in innovation. The experiences of successful entrepreneurs are shared, with the emphasis on the benefits of learning from failure. The underlying idea is that the best entrepreneurs are those who have failed and then overcome their failure by bouncing back financially, emotionally and professionally.

6. **Thinking "team" above all and prioritising cooperation.** Managers must take care not to constantly give prominence to themselves. They must remain humble and consider others as important to the effective running of the company. This involves demonstrating empathy and establishing trust in interpersonal relationships, and nourishing this trust and making it grow so that everyone feels that they are contributing to the team. Favouring cooperation also means taking a collaborative approach to looking for solutions. However, it never means apathetically accepting the consensus or being lax!

7. **Trying your best to remain positive,** because the manager's mood and attitude have a major influence on the people working with them. Be aware that this positive stance is contagious for your whole team.

8. **Establishing respect by example.** This is undoubtedly one of the most difficult points for a manager. Indeed, it requires you to be strict and practise on a daily basis. The manager must never forget that all their gestures, actions, attitudes or words are observed, analysed and

often imitated. They must consequently observe a kind of asceticism, as their honesty, ethics, fairness and sense of justice have to be exemplary to win the respect of their colleagues.

9. **Getting your hands dirty.** The manager must know how to take personal risks for their colleagues, as well as how to punish them when necessary. This attitude gives them legitimacy and makes employees feel safe.

10. **Knowing how to manage the loneliness of power.** A person who becomes a manager becomes the person with the most responsibility among their colleagues, and this does prove isolating. The danger lies in getting wrapped up in the thought that they arrived there alone. By extension, the person can come to believe that they can only climb the career ladder alone. Another risk is the development of imposter syndrome.

BEWARE OF IMPOSTER SYNDROME

This is to do with the inner thoughts of a manager who moves into a new position or takes on a new task in their current role. They often ask themselves whether the shoes they are stepping into are too big. They then see themselves as an imposter and live in fear of being unmasked. This syndrome affects 70% of high-potential individuals. Working on their professional development can provide valuable help, as it allows them to get to know themselves better and be clear about their assets and grey areas.

11. **Practising authenticity and congruence.** This involves aligning your thoughts, beliefs and behaviours. This attitude creates confidence and stability within teams, because the manager is giving a sign that they can be trusted.

12. **Developing a sense of humour.** Let's be honest: nature is not fair in this area. However, humour is important because it brings the team together and helps to resolve tensions: the managers who are gifted with it are very lucky! In spite of everything, do not be too quick to consider yourself devoid of any form of humour: it is a way of seeing things which can take many forms and may develop as the personality evolves.

THE PROCESS COMMUNICATION MODEL

The Process Communication Model (PCM) is a model of communication created in 1980 by the American psychiatrist Taibi Khaler (born in 1943) which aims to facilitate exchanges between individuals. It involves classifying personalities into different categories. Knowing these categories allows communication to be simplified and adapted to each personality. According to PCM, which is currently a very popular model, benevolent management is one of four management styles, along with autocratic, laissez-faire and democratic. The defining feature of benevolent management is that it is more concerned with the person than the task. It strengthens the bonds in a team and encourages interactions and a spirit of cooperation.

WHAT DOES IT INVOLVE?

What does caring involve as a course of action for managers? There is no hiding the fact that this stance is personally demanding, because it needs clear-sightedness with regard to how you work and relate to others. Through a more human and meaningful approach, it leads to congruence.

A more human approach

An increasing number of managers are realising that a more human approach produces better results. It allows them to motivate their teams more effectively and optimise their resources.

It involves above all recognising what makes a colleague valuable rather than highlighting their flaws – in short, changing your outlook. It is easy to understand that people work better when they feel respected.

THE PYGMALION EFFECT

When a worker is viewed with positivity and trust by their manager, they will find the motivation to progress and move forward. In short, if you see your colleagues as excellent, they have every chance of becoming excellent: this is known as the Pygmalion effect. Above all, you must adopt this benevolent outlook towards all your colleagues, not just the ones you get on well with.

The importance of meaning

Now, management is carried out in complex environments: it is imperative to move away from mechanical tools and linear causality in order to respond to day-to-day challenges. You must say goodbye to focusing on the problem with the aim of finding its causes and therefore someone to blame. Causality has given way to complexity, where several factors become mixed up and mutually influence each other, thus giving rise to uncertainty. Managers are constantly called upon to transform this anxiety into confidence: they become carriers of meaning. Faced with perpetual change, teams need to be told "why". Faced with contradictions and uncertainties, they naturally turn towards their manager to find coherence.

Congruence is the goal

It is worth remembering that congruence, or "walk the talk", is a concept from neuro-linguistic programming (NLP) and is inspired by the work of the American psychologist Carl Rogers (1902-1987). It is present when what I am, what I think, my values, what I feel, what I say and what I do are all aligned. It can be identified by the harmony between verbal and nonverbal signs. This alignment gives rise to authenticity and the state of a person described as "centred".

Congruence is worked on in the field of self-confidence, with a genuine inner transformation which gives a radiant poise. According to Rogers, it is a matter of the harmony between the awareness of one's needs and desires, and the expression that is given to them. This creates a healthy state of mind which is conducive to self-realisation and which encourages the interlocutor to get past their defence mechanisms to re-establish their own congruence.

ARE YOU CONGRUENT?

To find out if you are congruent, you can ask yourself the following questions with regard to the situation you are experiencing:

- Is it like me to say or do that?
- Do I feel good both mentally and physically when I say or do that?

Do not forget to carry out this exercise regularly, and trust what you are feeling.

In the end, workers judge their managers based on the reality of their behaviour and the consistency of their words and actions.

A FAST-GROWING MANAGEMENT STYLE

An increasing number of businesses are adopting caring management

On 13 November 2009, the French magazine *Psychologies* created the "Day of Kindness", then launched an "appeal for more caring at work". Currently, more than 300 companies of all sizes participate in this. They are committed to developing concrete actions based around three axes:

- giving meaning to the work of every employee;
- developing the quality of relationships and allowing everyone to coexist in harmony;
- ensuring the wellbeing of individuals.

We can mention, for example:

- Google Europe, for whom a managerial stance and working environment oriented towards wellbeing are at the heart of the definition of caring.
- The auditor and consultancy firm KPMG, which has put in place a chart of seven good practices for maintaining work-life balance and ten managerial behaviours which encourage respectful relationships.
- The French retailer Groupe Casino, which makes benevolence the base of its approach to human resources and aims to lead without causing stress. As such, an expert on stress trains managers on three main points: giving work meaning, fixing goals in line with what the person is capable of achieving, and developing recognition.

The virtuous circle for companies

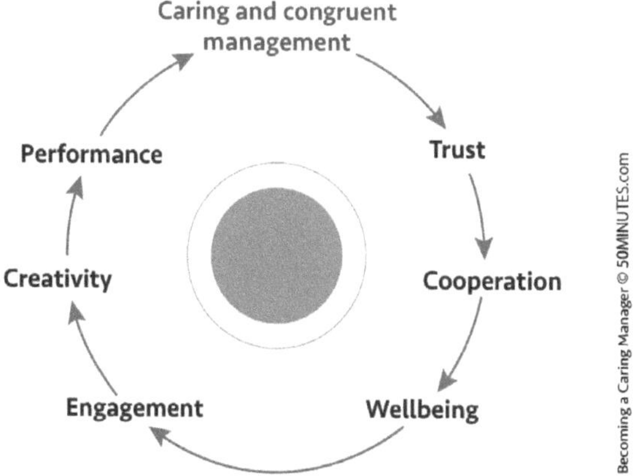

In short, benevolent and congruent management frees people's energy and talents. It is at once a response to current stress and a managerial approach that is suitable for all generations.

Suitability for intergenerational teams

Benevolent and congruent leadership responds perfectly to the current headache for managers, who complain of the gap between generations and the difficulty of uniting the increasing number of mixed teams.

First of all, it provides a solution to Generation Y's need for recognition and high-quality relationships (trust, good atmosphere, authenticity, etc.). It is also linked to their search for meaning, whether this involves their need to know why certain decisions or choices have been made, or their desire for self-development at work. Unlike Generation X, who had to demonstrate their competence, workers from Generation Y want their managers to trust them from the start, by setting up a trial period if necessary. They are constantly looking for information, and Generation X could play an important role in this, particularly in the transmission of professional expertise (for example through mentoring). By focusing on meaning, recognition and more relaxed relationships – points which members of Generation X will obviously not be opposed to – the manager allows each generation to find their place within the group.

Generation Z, who recently entered the world of work and see it as a jungle, know that they will hold several jobs and that most of the jobs of the future do not exist yet. Consequently, the company can learn from them, and the mix of generations provides a real opportunity to share knowledge. A successful caring manager has this openness and flexibility. They are able to manage these different paradigms because they know how to develop potential and stimulate synergies.

Extra information

A good way of immediately including colleagues from Generations Y and Z is to ask them for a confidential 'discovery report' from the first weeks after they arrive. This will focus on the six or eight points which most surprised them, as well as their proposals to improve them. It is then up to the manager to see which suggestions they can take on board.

Initial training

- The Department of Business Administration at France's Jean Monnet University offers a module on caring management, focusing on managing stress, as part of it Master's programme in Trade and Distribution Management.
- Since 2013, Rouen's university hospital has offered a training course in caring management for executives in the hospital setting with two flagship values, listening and the right to make mistakes, with a focus on the human aspects at the heart of management.
- Grenoble School of Management has included caring management in its list of thesis subjects for its doctoral course Doctorate of Business and Administration (DBA) since 2012.

At the same time, a number of consultancy, training and coaching firms across France, Belgium and Switzerland now offer training in caring management in response to the growing demand from businesses.

CONCLUSION

The time has come for the 'organic' management of companies, with less strict hierarchies and less reporting in order to encourage a greater focus on operations, with short management lines. The various current approaches each formulate, in their own way, this diversity of management focused on human relationships, because it is above all practiced by human beings towards their fellow human beings.

What makes caring and congruent management different is the fact that it leads to real relationships, which are more demanding than leaving the company opaque or remaining aloof. A caring and congruent manager is direct, open and positive, and they are brave enough to shake their staff up when they need it. They also have a pedagogical vocation, as they help their team to understand their successes and failures. They develop the talents of their colleagues as part of a dynamic that promotes progress. They are concerned about the wellbeing of other people, and are what the younger generation would call 'trustworthy', meaning that they are competent, caring, honest and consistent.

It bears repeating that this is a demanding management style for the manager, who must constantly work on themselves to develop their strength of character. There is no point hiding the fact that the first tool in the manager's arsenal is their own personality. Like any art form, it must be practiced regularly so that the technique ultimately disappears, leaving behind the rightness of the gesture.

Another distinctive feature of caring management is that it is still growing. This phase of major development still leaves adventurous managers the chance to broaden its territory themselves, and consequently to map the domain for their peers. By exploring unknown ground and casting light on shadowy areas, they can guide others to surpass their own limits.

Finally, as indicated by the AOM, the humanity of caring management means that it draws on approaches to management from all over the world, and the addition of the dimension of congruence makes it more open to the demands of tomorrow. We should not forget that the sphere of work is above all a place of life and a collective undertaking.

TOP TIPS

- Above all, never fake an interest in your employees: they will be able to tell straight away. Do not forget that 60-70% of communication is nonverbal. If you are not sincere, the tone of your voice, your posture and you face will give you away.

- Do not remind people at every opportunity that you are a caring manager. It is not about shouting it from the rooftops, but about fully embodying it by being congruent. This stance is gradually acquired and shaped, and once you have it, it will speak for itself. This type of manager can be identified very quickly.

- Cultivate your own wellbeing, because this influences your employees. Find your own way of revitalising yourself and boosting your energy – sports, mindfulness mediation, personal development, singing, theatre, etc. – and practice it regularly. Do not neglect your family life and social life: they play a part in your balance, which is essential because your state of mind has a knock-on effect on your team.

QUICK TRICK

A few minutes before you leave the office, write a few lines detailing your achievements for the day. Savour them for a few moments, then leave. This ritual will stop you from taking your stress home with you.

- Develop your emotional intelligence by listening to your own feelings. Welcome each emotion as a friend, because it is bringing a message about a need which has been satisfied or which needs to be satisfied. Our emotions function as an internal GPS which has the aim of helping us to respond to changes in our environment. It is usually said that there are six primary emotions (happiness, sadness, fear, surprise, disgust and anger) and, according to the American psychologist Paul Ekman (born in 1934), a pioneer in the study of emotions and their relationship with facial expressions, these are universal. It is useful for a manager to know what can trigger these emotions and what reactions they can lead to. Practising often will help you to develop this reflex. Once you have acquired it, it will allow you to identify your interlocutor's emotion and understand their behaviour. Consequently, you will then be able to adapt your own style of communication to theirs.

Emotions, their triggers and the reactions they cause

Emotion	Trigger	Reaction
Anger	Injustice or obstacle	Attack
Disgust	Harmful element	Rejection
Happiness	Success, positivity, achievement	Openness
Fear	Danger	Flight
Surprise	Unexpected situation	Withdrawal
Sadness	Loss	Withdrawal

Becoming a Caring Manager © 50MINUTES.com

FAQS

WHAT CAN I SAY TO PEOPLE WHO THINK THAT BEING CARING IS BEING NAÏVE?

A caring manager is not a doormat, a dreamer or a manipulator. They demonstrate respect and humanity on a daily basis to make their employees' jobs easier and reach their objectives. This does not stop them from saying things; rather, they try to say them well. Of course, it is often easier to lose your temper, to try to impose your will through force or threats, or to run away from your responsibilities: this is why being caring is a more demanding exercise for the manager who chooses this approach.

WHY SHOULD I CHOOSE A CARING MANAGEMENT STYLE DIRECTED TOWARDS CONGRUENCE?

There are a number of reasons for this, all of them centred on a greater sense of wellbeing and consequently on a more effective professional presence. First of all, with regard to the manager, this approach to management allows the person who uses it to act in a way that is consistent with their values, which is essential for their psychological harmony. Furthermore, colleagues will be listened to and respected more, and will work in a calmer environment. As a result, they will be more effective, perform better, suffer less from illness and be less susceptible to stress.

WHAT ARE THE THREE KEY INDICATORS OF A CARING AND CONGRUENT APPROACH TO MANAGEMENT?

A caring and congruent manager can be recognised first of all by their personality: their high level of self-confidence allows them to place their trust in other people. This base of confidence then means that the manager is open to caring and congruence. Finally, the keystone lies in the manager's enjoyment of their job, because liking their work breathes energy into both the manager and their team.

WHAT IS THE DIFFERENCE BETWEEN ETHICAL MANAGEMENT, SLOW MANAGEMENT AND MANAGEMENT-COACHING?

Ethical management, conceived by the Dutch professor Muel Kaptein in 2003, advocates authenticity, trustworthiness, communication skills and concern for the wellbeing of employees.

Slow management was modelled in 2004 by the German Heike Bruch and the Indian Sumantra Ghoshal. Initially, it was about reducing hierarchisation and the organisation of requests coming from multiple participants in the company, in contrast with so-called 'fast management'. It then extended to consider the re-evaluation of individuals and their wellbeing within the company.

The manager-coach incorporates coaching tools into their approach to management. These tools include different forms of listening, rephrasing, caring, questioning and silence.

These different approaches to management have in common the fact that they have the humanity and well-being of employees at their heart. Caring and congruent management goes further by adding a positive outlook on employees, a concern for the common interest and a coherence which uses interpersonal intelligence to unlock collective intelligence.

IS CARING A KEY TO HAPPINESS IN THE PROFESSIONAL WORLD?

A 2014 study by the Great Place to Work Institute revealed that only 30% of employees are happy to go to work.

France's *Institut national de la santé et de la recherche médicale* (National Institute of Health and Medical Research) calculates that the constant increase in unhappiness at work costs between 2.6% and 3.8% of GDP each year. These two studies argue for caring as a way of increasing employees' sense of wellbeing at work, which is a step towards happiness at work.

HOW CAN I BECOME A CARING AND CONGRUENT MANAGER?

A caring and congruent manager thinks about the human side of things. Consequently, to become that kind of manager, you should be able to consider each relationship and interaction as another learning opportunity. You need to ensure that your colleagues make progress while also making progress yourself. Having left behind the dominant/dominated dilemma, you will be in a position to get something back from your management, listen to feedback and use it to adjust your approach.

EXTRA INFORMATION

As soon as you feel uncomfortable or uneasy following an interaction with a colleague or in the face of a particular situation, ask yourself: what attitude would have been fairer for me and more caring for the other person? Little by little, you will develop reflexes for this. Don't forget that every time you learn something new, new neural pathways are created; it is repetition that consolidates these pathways until the new behaviour becomes a reflex.

CAN ALL MANAGERS BECOME CARING?

It would seem that not all personality types have the propensity or the desire to become caring and congruent managers. In the most widely-used personality classification tool in the world, the Myers-Briggs Type Indicator, of the four preferences of each personality, only one (Intuition-Feeling) sets up caring as a preferential factor. That means that this personality type will have an aptitude for this type of management, because they have a natural propensity for authenticity and empathy.

Of course, this does not mean that caring and congruent management is an insurmountable challenge for other personalities, but rather that they will have to make more effort to develop their caring side.

WHAT DO THE LATEST FINDINGS ABOUT THIS MANAGEMENT STYLE SAY?

The latest findings in this domain are primarily focused on the concepts of resonance and mirror neurons.

- The resonant leader: in any group of people, the leader has the greatest power of emotional influence. When they encourage a positive emotional atmosphere, this allows the best in everyone to come out. This is resonance. Recent research on the how the brain works has looked at the impact that the mood and actions of a manager have on the people they manage.
- Mirror neurons: your brain reacts to your own actions, but also to the actions of other people. This explains, for example, the phenomenon of emotional contagion. Thanks to our neurons, when another person makes a gesture, the same areas are activated in our brains as if we were carrying out the action ourselves. This discovery revolutionises our view of our relationship with other people and the world: all we have to do to understand the intentions of another person is pay attention to our own feelings and to the emotion generated in us by the other person's attitude, as explained by neuromanagement.

Managers who practise caring and congruence are aware

of the impact of their mood or their positioning on their team. They know that they must remain positive and make sure that their words, gestures and actions are consistent with each other. They measure the power of the resonance between their state of mind and the state of mind of their employees. They are also very attentive to their emotional state during any interaction, because any changes will inform them about the emotional state of their interlocutor through the mirror effect.

OVER TO YOU

THE RIGHT QUESTIONS

Being an authority figure within a group confers a symbolic power. The manager crystallises the projections of the people they manage: because of their status, team members ascribe skills or abilities to them that they do not necessarily have in reality. In order to avoid succumbing to this illusion and to carry out caring management by being congruent, ask yourself a few questions. Answer honestly, as this will help you to get a clearer view of your approach to management.

- Why am I a manager? What is the meaning of my professional duty?
- Do I feel like I belong here?
- Is this role in line with my goals in life?

WATCH OUT

Often, untrained managers unwittingly cause stress for their colleagues. The classic example of this is middle managers: dropped into positions that they are not equipped for, these newly promoted managers thought they had found their dream job, but are in reality unable to cope with this new situation. They then get by as well as they can, but often find themselves trapped in the Karpman drama triangle (a social model used in transactional analysis), as they alternate between the roles of victim, persecutor and rescuer, all the while remaining unable to take care of their teams. It bears repeating: management is a job that cannot be improvised.

Likewise, all managers must have a clear idea of the concepts of power, authority, hierarchy and legitimacy in order to avoid being a mere puppet.

- Power: power over or with other people?
- Authority: does it come with the title, or is it earned through respect?
- Hierarchy: am I comfortable with this notion?
- Legitimacy: who confers it?

OBSERVING AND KNOWING YOURSELF

Some managers do not realise the negative effect that their behaviour can have on their colleagues, and have no idea about the image they can convey. Nonetheless, this realisation is a vital step in any change. Start by becoming aware of your influence, then learn to make the best of it by relying on your strong points.

There are two ways of getting to know yourself better and being aware of your assets and areas for improvement: one involves being guided by others, while the other is undertaken alone with tools or activities.

- If you are working with others, there are methods based on words and on body language, as well as other methods which bring together these two approaches.

- If you are working alone, you must find tools that work for you, such as personality tests, mediation practices, martial arts, yoga or spirituality: all approaches are effective. It is up to you to find one that is suitable for what you are looking for. Don't forget that knowing yourself better also helps you to get to know others better.

BUILDING ON THE BASICS

Of course, it is not enough to 'graft' on a managerial theory for it to catch on: the whole body needs to accept it. It must become a way of operating and behaving, preferably embedded in and carried by the entire company. Experiment and hold onto what works for you. Rely on your strong points to test out other areas. If communication is one of your strengths, use it to help you with the rest: it will help you to be less afraid of making mistakes. Don't forget that from now on you can be more forgiving of mistakes, including your own.

THINGS TO REMEMBER

- Committing to change involves above all learning to unlearn!
- Management is an art, and is cultivated on a daily basis. Caring is a demanding behaviour, because you are making an effort for other people.

Finally, pay attention to what is around you and you will notice that this approach is developing. The managers who adopt it always leave an indelible mark on their teams, because they encourage lasting change wherever they work.

We want to hear from you!
Leave a comment on your online library
and share your favourite books on social media!

FURTHER READING

BIBLIOGRAPHY

- Barabel, M. and Meier, O. (2006) *Managéor*. Paris: Dunod.
- Bouvié, A. (2007) *Management et sciences cognitives*. Vendôme, Presses Universitaires de France.
- Brunel, V. (2014) *Les managers de l'âme*. Paris: La découverte.
- Chibane, K. (2015) *Le développement de l'intelligence émotionnelle des managers par le coaching*. Diplôme d'études supérieures universitaires thesis. Paris 8.
- Cornette de Saint Cyr, X. (2013) *Pratiquer la bienveillance*. Chêne-Bourg (Switzerland): Jouvence.
- Détrié, P. (2015) *Manager au XXIe siècle*. Paris: Eyrolles.
- Ennesser, J.-L. (2014) Le Neuromanagement, application concrète des neurones miroirs. *Les Échos*. [Online]. [Accessed 16 November 2016]. Available from: <http://archives.lesechos.fr/archives/cercle/2014/05/23/cercle_97921.htm>
- Girard, A. (2013) Qu'est-ce qu'un management bienveillant ? *Seenago*. [Online]. [Accessed 16 November 2016]. Available from: <http://www.seenago.com/pdf/Questcequunmanagementbienveillant.pdf>
- Goleman, D., Boyatzis, R. and McKee, A. (2004) *Primal Leadership: Learning to Lead with Emotional Intelligence*. Massachusetts: Harvard Business School Press.
- Heinz, M. (2015) Signaling cooperation. *Social Science Research Network*. [Online]. [Accessed 17 November 2016]. Available from: <http://papers.ssrn.com/sol3/

papers.cfm?abstract_id=2696911>

- Kotsou, I. (2015) *Intelligence émotionnelle et management.* Louvain-la-Neuve (Belgium): De Boeck.
- Lenhardt, V. (2003) *Coaching for Meaning: The Culture and Practice of Coaching and Team Building.* London: Palgrave Macmillan.
- Obéa (2014) Les salariés des grandes entreprises françaises et le capital humain. *Slideshare.* [Online]. [Accessed 17 November 2016]. Available from: <http:// fr.slideshare.net/MichaelPageFrance/1542-mp-frabrochurebookletweb-36340928>
- Mantione, F. (No date) Le management bienveillant : sujet, verbe, compliment. *Florian Mantione Institut.* [Online]. [Accessed 17 November 2016]. Available from: <http://www.florianmantione.com/actualites/edi-tos/247-le-management-bienveillant-sujet-verbe-com-pliment>
- Mutuelle Bleue (No date). Pour un management par la bienveillance. *Mutuelle Bleue.* [Online]. [Accessed 17 November 2016]. Available from: <http://www. mutuellebleue.fr/actu-et-prevention/incollableu/ pour-un-management-par-la-bienveillance>
- Schutz, W. (1994) *The Human Element: Productivity, Self-Esteem and the Bottom Line.* California: Jossey Bass.
- Sève, M.-M. (2011) Sept clés pour manager avec bienveillance. *L'Express Entreprise.* [Online]. [Accessed 17 November 2016]. Available from: <http://lentreprise. lexpress.fr/rh-management/sept-cles-pour-manager-avec-bienveillance_1518872.html>
- Soudy, E. (2011) Management bienveillant. *Eric Soudy.* [Online]. [Accessed 17 November 2016]. Available

from: <https://sites.google.com/site/airhikzen/
management-equitable/managementbienveillant>

- Steiler, D., Sadowsky, J. and Roche, L. (2010) *Éloge du bien-être au travail.* Grenoble: Presses Universitaires de Grenoble.
- Tanquerel, S. (2014) Oser le management bienveil-lant. *Le Journal des grandes écoles et universités.* [Online]. [Accessed 17 November 2016]. Available from: <http://journaldesgrandesecoles.com/oser-le-management-bienveillant%C2%A0/>
- Tournant, J. (2014) *La stratégie de la bienveillance ou l'intelligence de la coopération.* Paris: InterÉditions.
- Trehorel, L. (2015) Se former au "management bienveil-lant". *Action Co.* [Online]. [Accessed 17 November 2016]. Available from: <http://www.actionco.fr/Thematique/management-1020/Breves/Developpement-formation-management-bienveillant-259903.htm#.VplqAvnhA4Y>
- Vittori, J.-M. (2015) Quand les entreprises embaucheront des cœurs. *Les Échos.* [Online]. [Accessed 17 November 2016]. Available from: <http://www.lesechos.fr/idees-debats/editos-analyses/021620697193-quand-les-entreprises-embaucheront-des-coeurs-1192532.php>

ADDITIONAL SOURCES

- Bandler, R. and Grinder, J. (1989) *The Structure of Magic I: A Book About Language and Therapy.* California: Science and Behavior Books.
- Bandler, R. and Grinder, J. (1989) *The Structure of Magic II.* California: Science and Behavior Books.
- Boyatzis, R.E. and McKee, A. (2005) *Resonant Leadership.*

Renewing Yourself and Connecting with Others Through Mindfulness, Hope and Compassion. Boston: Harvard Business School Press.

- Ramachandran, V. (2003) *The Emerging Mind*. London: Profile Books.
- Rizzolatti, G. and Signigaglia, C. (2007) *Mirrors in the Brain: How Our Minds Share Actions and Emotions*. Oxford: Oxford University Press.
- Rogers, C. (2004) *On Becoming a Person*. London: Constable & Robinson Ltd.

IMPROVE YOUR
GENERAL KNOWLEDGE
IN A BLINK OF AN EYE !

www.50minutes.com

© 50MINUTES.com, 2016. All rights reserved.

www.50minutes.com

Ebook EAN: 9782806289087

Paperback EAN: 9782806291516

Legal Deposit: D/2016/12603/887

Cover: © Primento

Digital conception by Primento, the digital partner of publishers.